YoungWriters

GW01390075

My First Acrostic

The South West Of England

Edited by Jenni Bannister

First published in Great Britain in 2011 by:

YoungWriters

Remus House
Coltsfoot Drive
Peterborough
PE2 9BF
Telephone: 01733 890066
Website: www.youngwriters.co.uk

All Rights Reserved
© Copyright Contributors 2011
SB ISBN 978-0-85739-465-1

Foreword

The 'My First Acrostic' collection was developed by Young Writers specifically for Key Stage 1 children. The poetic form is simple, fun and gives the young poet a guideline to shape their ideas, yet at the same time leaves room for their imagination and creativity to begin to blossom.

Due to the young age of the entrants we have enjoyed rewarding their effort by including as many of the poems as possible. Our hope is that seeing their work in print will encourage the children to continue writing as they grow and develop their skills into our poets of tomorrow.

Young Writers was established in 1990 to nurture creativity in our children and young adults, to give them an interest in poetry and an outlet to express themselves. This latest collection will act as a milestone for the young poets and one that will be enjoyable to revisit again and again.

Contents

The Abbey CE (VA) Primary School, Shaftesbury

Trythall Community Primary School, New Mill

Wellesley Park Primary School, Wellington

The Poems

The Octopus

O wen octopus

W iggled his legs

E very day at sea

N ear the sand

B y a rock.

Owen Brightman (5)
Archbishop Wake Primary School, Blandford Forum

Golden Eagle

G olden

O ld, been there for years

L oving

D aring to race

E lephant

N early extinct

E agle

A bominable golden eagle

G olden

L eaping to fly

E ats fish and other things.

Leah Crabbe (6)
Archbishop Wake Primary School, Blandford Forum

Elephant

E agles fly

L ollipops melt

E ggs you eat

P eople snore

H orses run

A nts crawl

N ewspaper people read

T ennis balls people hit.

Sasha Payne (6)
Archbishop Wake Primary School, Blandford Forum

Fighting Fit

S isters and brothers.

H ealthy.

A s ourselves.

Z ip go our shoes.

Shahzaib Saleem (6)
Archbishop Wake Primary School, Blandford Forum

Giraffe

G erbils are funny pets

I 'm interested in big bird nests

R abbits are in the field jumping

A eroplanes are flying high in the sky

F ish are gold fish

F ish fingers are tasty to eat

E lephants are fat and greedy.

Sophie Snape (6)
Archbishop Wake Primary School, Blandford Forum

Acrostic Poem - Giraffe

G iraffes are tall

I n the clouds

R ising high in the sky

A s they go

F ar in the sky

F ar as they can go

E ars high in the sky.

Jessica Andrews (6)
Archbishop Wake Primary School, Blandford Forum

Kayleigh

K ind

A nd eating a banana

Y ellow hair

L isten

E ating apples

I like playing

G ood girl

H elping Mummy.

Kayleigh Eva Frampton (5)
Archbishop Wake Primary School, Blandford Forum

Archie

A rchie plays with his Action Man.

R aces cars.

C uddle my crocodile.

H as a wrestling box.

I am six.

E very Thursday and Friday I eat burgers.

Archie Miller (6)
Archbishop Wake Primary School, Blandford Forum

Rowan

R owan is seven

O nly does tidying once in a while

W hen I feel like it

A nd that is not often

N ever let my friends down, especially Hollie.

Rowan Alice Haines (7)
Archbishop Wake Primary School, Blandford Forum

Florrie

F lowery Florrie loves watching TV

L ovely golden hair.

O ften I go for long walks.

R oses are my favourite flowers.

R ed roses in the garden.

I like playing with my friends.

E very rainbow in the sky makes me very happy.

Florrie Hansen (6)
Archbishop Wake Primary School, Blandford Forum

Ethan

E than is a boy

T akes Murphy for walks

H as a pet snail

A lways help Daddy

N ice to my friends.

Ethan Drewett (6)
Archbishop Wake Primary School, Blandford Forum

School

S afe school

C lass 3

H as fun

O ur class is the best

O ur class is good

L ove Class 3.

Katie Robinson (5)
Bishop Bronescombe CE (VA) School, St Austell

6

Beach

B each sandcastles

E verywhere

A t the beach there are ice cream vans

C an you splash?

H ave fun.

Keedi Hawke (5)
Bishop Bronescombe CE (VA) School, St Austell

Chinese

C hinese dragon

H ot sun

I like Chinese food

N ot Chinese food with fish though

E lephants with patterns

S urrounded by people

E verybody different.

Bayley Walsh (6)
Bishop Bronescombe CE (VA) School, St Austell

Home

H ome is fun

O n and off at home

M y home is great

E veryone has fun.

Joshua Robinson (6)
Bishop Bronescombe CE (VA) School, St Austell

Bat

B ats flying in the sky

A bat sucks blood

T hey are scary.

Isaac Foot (5)
Bishop Bronescombe CE (VA) School, St Austell

Beach

B irds flying

E ating lollies

A sea making waves

C an you swim?

H ot day.

Chelsey Trudgian (5)
Bishop Bronescombe CE (VA) School, St Austell

Dogs

D oggy biscuits

O utside running

G o fetch the toy

S o cuddly.

Milli Hughes (5)
Bishop Bronescombe CE (VA) School, St Austell

Brother

B ig boy helps me

R eads me stories

O n the sofa

T hank you boy

H elping me with spellings

E ating tea with me

R eally kind to me.

Sarah Oshin (5)
Bishop Bronescombe CE (VA) School, St Austell

Bat

B ats are good

A lways sleeping upside down

T hey fly at night.

Louis Edyvean (6)
Bishop Bronescombe CE (VA) School, St Austell

Beach

B eaches are fun

E very summer

A t the beach I have an ice cream

C lass 3 can come next time and enjoy the

H ot sun.

Keylee Rowe (6)
Bishop Bronescombe CE (VA) School, St Austell

School

S uper school

C lass 3 is here

H andwriting is good

O ur class is good

O ur class is fun

L ovely Class 3.

Tegan Roberts (6)
Bishop Bronescombe CE (VA) School, St Austell

Beach

B all games

E ating ice cream

A beach is fun

C old sea

H ot sun.

Lewis Toms (6)
Bishop Bronescombe CE (VA) School, St Austell

Beach

B each is fun

E ating picnics

A nd building sandcastles

C rashing waves

H ot sun.

Ebony Cole (5)
Bishop Bronescombe CE (VA) School, St Austell

Home

H ome is good

O h home you are great

M um bakes cakes

E ating tasty cakes.

Emmy Lovegrove (6)
Bishop Bronescombe CE (VA) School, St Austell

Edward

E xtremely good.

D ancing I am good at!

W inning at snooker.

A mazing at maths.

R acing against Ellie.

D ogs I don't like.

Edward Brain (7)
Blundell's Preparatory School, Tiverton

All About Me

B eautiful Bethany.

E ats sweets.

T ickles people.

H as a cat.

A t school I have fun.

N aughty Bethany.

Y oung and lovely.

K ind girl.

E legant Bethany.

E ats fruit.

D oes naughty things at home.

W hen I go on holiday.

E ats cakes.

L oves things like animals.

L oves friends.

Bethany Keedwell (6)
Blundell's Preparatory School, Tiverton

All About Me

T ickles Mum and Dad

H as a Wii that you play on

O nce I jumped over a high wall

M unches carrots and potatoes

A good rugby player and football player

S miley every day, I am so smiley

L ovely Thomas

A strong Thomas

B ooks around my house

D ick King Smith is my favourite author

O nce I went on my skateboard and squashed a mouse

N oisy around my house.

Thomas Labdon (6)
Blundell's Preparatory School, Tiverton

All About Me

E ats fruit

S neaks up on my younger sister, Amber

T hinks a lot about maths

E ats sweets

L oves sweets

L oves swimming

E njoys Ferris wheels

T hinks a lot about animals

U sually does mental maths

C ooks yummy cakes

K ind and cute

E ats cakes

R osy cheeks.

Estelle Tucker (6)
Blundell's Preparatory School, Tiverton

Alice

A lways happy

L ikes playing with Eve

I s good at eating pepper with hummus

C ake eater

E xcellent at playing on my DS

W ish for sunny days

I s cheerful

L oves school

L oves doing my work

I s funny

A scaredy-cat

M ust go to school

S miles a lot.

Alice Williams (6)
Blundell's Preparatory School, Tiverton

Jessica Payne

J elly is one of my favourite foods.

E xcited on birthdays.

S uper at mopping.

S pecial to my mummy.

I love my family.

C ats are one of my favourite pets.

A crobatic at sports.

P erfect at ballet.

A mazing at maths.

Y ou tell me what to do - I'll do it.

N umber facts are easy.

E xcellent at spelling tests.

Jessica Payne (7)
Blundell's Preparatory School, Tiverton

Finlay

F abulous me.

I am good at fixing cars.

N ice to my friends.

L ove going outside.

A mazing at football.

Y ummy pasta I like.

Finlay Williams (6)
Blundell's Preparatory School, Tiverton

Amelia-Rose

A mazing at everything.

M aths is my favourite.

E nergetic at everything.

L ovely in every way.

I love my family.

A crobatic at sport.

–

R esponsible me.

O nly good, never naughty.

S uper sporty.

E xpressive with my reading.

Amelia-Rose Richards (7)
Blundell's Preparatory School, Tiverton

Nathan White

N aughty to my sisters.

A lways good at sport.

T errific at rugby.

H enry is my friend.

A ngry at home.

N ot nice to my parents.

W onderful at maths.

H orrible at home.

I love chocolate.

T ry my best.

E xcellent at cricket.

Nathan White (7)
Blundell's Preparatory School, Tiverton

Red Riding Hood

R osy cheeks dimpling,

E agerly skipping through the woods,

D anger skulking behind the trees.

R ed cloak swinging

I n time to her skips.

D aring to leave the path,

I nto her basket go armfuls of bluebells.

N asty wolf runs on ahead,

G ranny locked in the wardrobe.

H airy wolf in the bed,

O ld lady, but with big sharp teeth.

O h dear!

D oor bursts open and here is the woodcutter.

Hedgemoor Class (5-7)
Christow School, Christow

Adam

A dam likes Alfie

D izzy dummies

A mazing

M agical.

Adam Thomas (7)
East Huntspill School, Highbridge

Nathan

N ice
A mazing
T remendous
H appy
A dventurous
N osy.

Nathan Fey (5)
East Huntspill School, Highbridge

Sydney Huett

S nuggly
Y oung
D elightful
N ice
E xcitable
Y o-yoing

H uggable
U ntidy
E xperimental
T op girl
T icklish.

Sydney Huett (7)
East Huntspill School, Highbridge

Destiny Clement

D angerous

E xperimental

S trong

T icklish

I ntelligent

N ippy

Y oung

C lever

L ovely

E ntertaining

M onkey

E njoyable

N ice

T all.

Destiny Clement (7)
East Huntspill School, Highbridge

Ethan

E xcited

T errific

H appy

A mazing

N eat.

Ethan Lukins (5)
East Huntspill School, Highbridge

Josh

J umping jelly

O ver-excited

S nuggly

H appy.

Josh Harvey (5)
East Huntspill School, Highbridge

Rhiannon

R eally very cheeky

H appy as can be

I s very, very lovely

A nd is pretty and giggly

N osy and curious

N oisy too

O thers really like her

N ow won't you?

Rhiannon Metcalf (5)
Emmanuel School, Exeter

Elephant

E legant and enchanting

L arge and lovely

E xotic and endearing

P atient and pretty

H uge

A frican or Indian

N ature's giants

T runks and tusks.

Owen Hensher (4)
Falmouth Primary School, Falmouth

Tractors

T ractors are the farmer's best friend

R ough or smooth, the tractor doesn't mind

A nd animals need help to feed them too

C ome inside and have a ride and see what animals we can find

T railers are pulled by the tractor to carry heavy loads

O range, red, green and blue, that's the colours of them too

R ev, rev the tractor goes, around the fields all day long

S ome days are rainy, some days are sunny, but whatever the
weather the tractor is running.

Harvey Hutchings (6)
Falmouth Primary School, Falmouth

Tiger

T imid but strong

I ntriguing but respected

G reedy and messy

E legant and soft

R ed and white.

Nathan Saunders (4)
Falmouth Primary School, Falmouth

Miss Norman

M iss Norman

I s my teacher

S he teaches us lots

S he is always happy

N ever sad

O n Friday she

R eally

M akes us laugh

A nd we

N ever want to leave school.

Kimberley Jenkin (6)
Falmouth Primary School, Falmouth

Hobs

H obs has paws

O utside he sleeps

B ees

S ometimes he catches them.

Dexter McCullough (5)
Falmouth Primary School, Falmouth

Hello Kitty

H ello Kitty wears a pink dress

E veryone

L oves Hello Kitty

L ots of days I see her

O n television

K itty is her sister

I n her house

T he family loves Hello Kitty

T hey always go out

Y ou might see her.

Lauren Heidstrom (6)
Falmouth Primary School, Falmouth

Amber

A mber is cute

M y bones are strong

B ows in my hair

E veryone is my friend

R eally like my dad.

Amber Symonds (5)
Falmouth Primary School, Falmouth

Miss Norman

Miss Norman is my teacher

I like her a lot

She is always happy

She always makes me laugh

Now I can't wait to go to school

On Monday, Tuesday, Wednesday, Thursday and Friday

Rainy days or sunny days are

My favourite school days

And I can't wait to see Miss

Norman every day!

Dion Cooke (6)
Falmouth Primary School, Falmouth

JLS

Just love singing

Lots of singing

Singing all day long!

Freya Edney (5)
Falmouth Primary School, Falmouth

Kittens

K ittens are baby cats

I have a kitten

T hey like to play

T hey sleep lots and lots

E very day

N ow my kitten will

S oon be a cat.

Kairi Rowe (6)
Falmouth Primary School, Falmouth

Cats

C ats are snuggly

A nd cute

T he cat is playful

S ometimes they are scared.

Quentin Johnson-Hosking (6)
Falmouth Primary School, Falmouth

Flowers, Flowers

F lowers, flowers
L ots of flowers
O n my lawn
W hen I go outside
E very day I see
R eally colourful flowers
S top and see!

Demelza Kelly (6)
Falmouth Primary School, Falmouth

JLS

J LS rock
L et's sing their songs
S mile and dance.

Alfie Haith (5)
Falmouth Primary School, Falmouth

Body

B odies are important

O ur bodies let us move

D o you know that you have 206 bones in

Y our body?

Daisy May (5)
Falmouth Primary School, Falmouth

Orange

O range is round like a ball

R ed like an apple

A flower is growing out of the ground

N othing can stop them now

G rass is growing too big

E veryone has a bit of a rest.

Alice Keyte (6)
Flax Bourton CE Primary School, Flax Bourton

Blueberry

B ursting blueberry

L ike a volcano

U p in the sky it is hard to see

E at them all up

B lue like the sky

E veryone is yummy

R ound as a circle

R oll them all around

Y ummy blueberry.

Libby Bayliss (7)
Flax Bourton CE Primary School, Flax Bourton

Carrot

C runchy orange fruit

A ll yummy and bumpy

R ocky and extremely juicy

R umbling in your stomach

O n the tasty side

T he scrummy vegetable is very creamy.

Emma Armstrong (6)
Flax Bourton CE Primary School, Flax Bourton

Banana

B rown rotten banana

A very good banana

N asty banana

A good banana

N oble banana

A very good healthy banana.

Alfie Sheahan (6)
Flax Bourton CE Primary School, Flax Bourton

Carrot

C rackly and crackly

A ngry and tasty

R ock hard

R ocky hard

O ctopus arms

T asty and yummy.

Sergio Basma (6)
Flax Bourton CE Primary School, Flax Bourton

Grapes

G rapes are yummy

R ed grapes are yummy

A ngry and furious

P ick the grapes

E at them

S lithery.

Isabelle Moore (6)
Flax Bourton CE Primary School, Flax Bourton

Grapes

G rapes grow on the tree.

R eally yummy on the tree.

A berry can't be so yummy.

P ut them in a bowl.

E xplain it and eat it.

S omething can't be yummy.

Hazel Moon Clark (7)
Flax Bourton CE Primary School, Flax Bourton

Cat

C limb
A lways go out
T ickle tummy.

Zoe Haines (4)
Hayesdown First School, Frome

Alien

A re green
L ive on the moon
I love aliens
E njoy laughing
N ice.

Joel Sansom (5)
Hayesdown First School, Frome

Horse

H ooves

O ver fences

R iders wear hats

S it on the saddle

E at carrots.

Milly Applegate (4)
Hayesdown First School, Frome

Dog

D og pound

O n four legs

G round.

Sam Carver (5)
Hayesdown First School, Frome

Pig

P laying in mud

I like piggies

G runt.

Fraya Rodgers (4)
Hayesdown First School, Frome

Rosie

R un

O ranges

S miley

I write nicely

E at sandwiches.

Rosie Butler (4)
Hayesdown First School, Frome

Alien

A ll blue

L ittle

I n space

E yes

N aughty.

Jake Wason (5)
Hayesdown First School, Frome

Animals

A nt

N asty bats

I like rabbits

M ole

A nteater

L adybird.

Katy Peniket (4)
Hayesdown First School, Frome

Lorry

L ots of noise

O n the road

R oars

R eally big

Y ellow.

Morgan Doel (5)
Hayesdown First School, Frome

Dog

D rinks water

O ften eats

G oes to the kennels.

Courtneigh Meadows (5)
Hayesdown First School, Frome

Cars

C olourful
A red one
R eally fast
S pecial.

Ben Pearse (4)
Hayesdown First School, Frome

Cat

C atches
A mouse
T hen sleeps.

Keira Morgan (5)
Hayesdown First School, Frome

Fire

F ireworks

I n the house

R ing 999

E verywhere.

Samantha Hurd (5)
Hayesdown First School, Frome

Train

T unnel

R unning

A nd fun

I n a station

N ice whistle.

Gareth Everton (5)
Hayesdown First School, Frome

Cake

C hocolate
A nd silver balls
K itchen surface
E at them up.

Charlie Evans (5)
Hayesdown First School, Frome

Pirate

P eter Pan
I n the sea
R ed hat
A bandon ship
T he goodies got killed
E very pirate has a cloak.

Benjamin Fleming (5)
Hayesdown First School, Frome

Flowers

F rom the shop
L ovely
O range
W ater
E veryone
R ed
S eeds.

Thomas Harrison (4)
Hayesdown First School, Frome

Cat

C alled Benjy
A nd is black and white
T he back garden.

Melissa Carbine (4)
Hayesdown First School, Frome

Caitlyn Le Bretton

C ycling is fun

A mazing

I like ice cream

T all

L oving

Y oung

N ice

L ovely

E xciting

B rave

R ats are horrid

E aster is my favourite time

T alkative

T ickling

O utrageous

N ice.

Caitlyn Le Bretton (7)
Heamoor Community Primary School, Heamoor

Lewis Williams

L ovely
E xcited
W arm
I nterested
S lippers

W eak
I ndian
L azy
L arge
I ncredible
A liens
M unchy
S ad.

Lewis Williams (7)
Heamoor Community Primary School, Heamoor

Kamile Ruibyte

K is the first letter of my name.

A mazing game that I play.

M aisie and Ellie are my best friends.

I love school.

L ady GaGa's songs are my favourite songs.

E ggs are lovely.

R uth is my friend.

U nder my bed there's my kite.

I like apples.

B ikes are brilliant.

Y ucky custard but I like it.

T ug of war is my game.

E verything is right in my life.

Kamile Ruibyte (6)
Heamoor Community Primary School, Heamoor

Tia Murray-Lambrou

T igers are my favourite animals.

I try to do my best in school.

A frica is my favourite place.

M ummy is my favourite in the family.

U gly rats are not nice to me.

R epeating birds are my favourite.

R oaring animals are the best.

A nimals are marvellous things.

Y ummy food is great.

Tia Murray-Lambrou (7)
Heamoor Community Primary School, Heamoor

Millie Mead

M y brother is annoying.

I like ice cream.

L azy daddy.

L ollipops are my favourite food.

I love my mummy.

E ggs are my favourite food.

M y toys were exciting.

E lephants have long trunks.

A bove the sky.

D iving is the best.

Millie Mead (6)
Heamoor Community Primary School, Heamoor

Ellie Dash

E lephants are one of my best animals.

L ollipops are tasty for me.

L oopy and enthusiastic.

I like riding my bike.

E xciting books are good.

D ashing is what I do best.

A pples are my favourite fruit.

S nakes are the worst animals at the zoo.

H ouses are warm for me and my sister.

Ellie Dash (7)
Heamoor Community Primary School, Heamoor

47

Isaac Trevains

I like school.

S ome dogs have sharp teeth.

A child is silly.

A cat is cute.

C hris is my dad.

T ug of war is hard.

R ude.

E vil rats are naughty.

V ans are white.

A birthday is exciting.

I love my family.

N oisy.

S unny days are nice days.

Isaac Trevains (6)
Heamoor Community Primary School, Heamoor

Ella Wood

E lephants are cool.

L ollipops are my favourite thing.

L ions are brilliant because they roar.

A nts are tiny and I like them.

W e made our marvellous medicine yesterday.

O lives are yucky because they make me feel sick.

O n my birthday I had lots of presents.

D ogs are great because you can stroke them.

Ella Wood (7)
Heamoor Community Primary School, Heamoor

48

Izzy Graham

I mpressive

Z igzag

Z ang

Y ucky

G alloping

R idiculous

A ggressive

H appy

A crobatic

M ad.

Izzy Graham (6)
Heamoor Community Primary School, Heamoor

Rhys Wiseman

R acing around on a go-kart is fun.

H ot dogs are my favourite food.

Y appy all the time at home.

S un lover.

W ould like to be a vet.

I 've got a sister.

S illy.

E xcited.

M eowy is my favourite teddy.

A ctivity lover.

N oisy.

Rhys John Wiseman-Watkins (7)
Heamoor Community Primary School, Heamoor

49

Sienna Thomas

S unny

I nteresting

E xcited

N oisy

N ice

A ngry

T ired

H orsey

O ptimistic

M oody

A mazing

S urprising.

Sienna Thomas (7)
Heamoor Community Primary School, Heamoor

Charlie Edwards

C ats are boring.

H ats are better than crocodiles.

A nimals are cool.

R ats are cool.

L ollies are my best food.

I like ice cream.

E lephants are good to me.

E lla is a good friend.

D inosaurs are my favourite beasts.

W oody is the funniest cowboy.

A pples are good fantastic food.

R ats are good animals.

D addy is my greatest dad.

S aturday is my best day.

Charlie Edwards (6)
Heamoor Community Primary School, Heamoor

Maisie Reed

My kitten is called Noodle.

Ants are great.

I don't like rats.

Sweets are delicious.

I made marvellous medicine yesterday.

Elephants are cool.

Rats are horrid.

Eggs are yummy.

Elephants are massive compared to me.

Dad is very tall.

Maisie Reed (7)
Heamoor Community Primary School, Heamoor

Seth Arthur

Smiling

Excited

Ticklish

Hungry

Argumentative

Rainbow

Talented

Huggy

Unbelievable

Red.

Seth Arthur (6)
Heamoor Community Primary School, Heamoor

William Tuckett

W ii

I like playing on the Wii

L ucky

L ike ice cream

I ce

A mazing

M e

T ricky

U neasy

C heerful

K ind

E xcited

T idy

T oys.

William Tuckett (7)
Heamoor Community Primary School, Heamoor

Mollie Maycock

M agic

O utrageous

L azy

L ively

I ll

E xcited

M arvellous

A crobat

Y awning

C razy

O dd

C olourful

K ind.

Mollie Maycock (6)
Heamoor Community Primary School, Heamoor

Ismay Cornish

I like riding my horse.

S ometimes I fight with my brother.

M onday is my favourite day.

A nimals are great.

Y ellow is my favourite colour.

C ats are boring.

O ranges are sort of nice.

R uth is a good friend.

N othing is better than riding my horse.

I like ice cream.

S tables are where my horse sleeps.

H orses are my favourite animals.

Ismay Cornish (7)
Heamoor Community Primary School, Heamoor

Taila Jade Simmonds

T easing
A ngry
I nteresting
L ively
A rtistic

J olly
A ble
D ark
E xcellent.

Taila Jade Simmonds (6)
Heamoor Community Primary School, Heamoor

Shark Poem

S harks seem to fight,
H umpback whales chase them,
A re always chasing them,
R eally big teeth,
K ill fish to eat,
S ee how many sharks you can see.

Joe Trapani (6)
Hillside First School, Worle

The Starfish

S tarfish have five legs,

T hey grow back legs,

A starfish lives in the coral,

R ays hurt them,

F ish are friends with them,

I think they are pretty,

S tarfish feel bumpy,

H ow they stick to rocks!

Elise Vernon-Mason (6)
Hillside First School, Worle

Dolphin Poem

D olphins live in the sea near the shore.

O ut in the sea jump the dolphins.

L isten, hear the dolphins squeak.

P eople swim with them.

H ope you like my poem so far.

I n the water they swim.

N ow see the dolphins swim in the water.

S o this fact is nice, a female gives the baby its milk underwater.

Emily Poynton (7)
Hillside First School, Worle

Whale Poem

Whales eat the other fish.

Have a big mouth.

Always swim.

Long.

Everyone hears them.

Ethan Hawley (6)
Hillside First School, Worle

Crab Poem

Crawling along on the dry sand.

Round the beach they go.

A crab has a shell.

Big crabs look big and scary.

Matthew Morris (6)
Hillside First School, Worle

Shark Poem

S harks eat fish and have sharp teeth

H ave three gills on each side to breathe

A mako shark is slim and speedy

R ips tuna and mackerel and has very sharp teeth

K ills its prey and eats it.

Kallum Bobbin (6)
Hillside First School, Worle

Fish Poem

F ish live in the sea

I n the sea they are different colours

S parkly gills and scales

H ave wavy fins.

Liam Rogers (7)
Hillside First School, Worle

Fish Poem

F ins and gills.

I love fish because we can eat them.

S hiny scales.

H ave no smooth skin.

Millie-Lou Baker (7)
Hillside First School, Worle

Fish Poem

F ish have flippers and fins

I n the sea they swim. In the great sea

S ee all the different colours and fish

H ave shiny scales.

Abby Flourentzou (7)
Hillside First School, Worle

Shells

S hells are still in the sand.

H ere are some shells.

E very shell looks big and small.

L ittle shells spread around.

L ittle shells all around.

S hells which are bumpy.

Christine Shibu (7)
Hillside First School, Worle

Seashell

S mooth to touch

H ow I love to see them shine

E very time I try to touch, oh it is so smooth

L ike the way the sun shines on the shell

L ike the way you touch a shell.

Isabelle Grayston (7)
Hillside First School, Worle

61

Dolphin Poem

D olphins are blue, dolphins have wet tails.

O pen their mouths to eat.

L ittle dolphins born from their mothers.

P eople look at them while they do tricks.

H ave very smooth skin.

I n the water they swim.

N ow the poem is finished.

Lucy Frost (7)
Hillside First School, Worle

Fish Poem

F ish are different colours

I n the sea they go

S ee the fish swim

H ave shiny scales.

Owen Jenkins (6)
Hillside First School, Worle

Shark Poem

S ee sharks going by.

H ave smooth bodies.

A shark has sharp teeth.

R ight in the sea see the sharks swimming.

K eep away because sharks are dangerous.

Erin Hale (6)
Hillside First School, Worle

Dolphins

D olphins are very big.

O n some occasions dolphins sing.

L ow and high the dolphins glide.

P aying no attention to other fish.

H e would go and splash about.

I t would be sometimes blue.

N ice little dolphins love the sea.

S plashing around the dolphins will go.

Brooke Hester (7)
Hillside First School, Worle

Ethan

E than is a boy

T errible thinker

H air is brown

A lways active

N aughty sometimes.

Ethan Durward (7)
Hillside First School, Worle

Dolphin

D olphins are nice to humans sometimes.

O ther dolphins are big or small.

L ive dolphins come to you or not.

P lease do not frighten the dolphins.

H is fins are big or small.

I nside is a hole for their nose.

N ever touch a dolphin if it's bad.

Eve Bennett (7)
Hillside First School, Worle

My First Acrostic 2011 - The South West Of England

Shark

S harks have sharp teeth.

H ope you never get eaten by one.

A shark has two beady eyes.

R are sharks are the great white sharks.

K iller sharks come to eat you.

Josh Beattie (7)
Hillside First School, Worle

Dolphins

D ive in the sea.

O ut of the sea creatures

L eap in and out the water.

P uff in air from human Earth.

H igh leaps in the air.

I n water animals.

N ever be unkind to humans.

Caitlin Ashurst (7)
Hillside First School, Worle

65

Shark

S harks are grey and white.

H ot sharks have sharp teeth

A nd sharks eat fish.

R un, sharks go fast.

K iller sharks can kill you.

Codey Spearing (6)
Hillside First School, Worle

Great White Shark

G reat white shark is big and fat.

R eally long body.

E at, eat, eat goes the shark.

A great white shark is known for its nastiness.

T errible jaws snap all day.

W e will like it or we won't.

H e or she might think we are turtles.

I t could be nice or nasty.

T wo will make a noise.

E at everything in their path.

S he will soon love a he.

H e will make a noise to see her.

A great white hunts any kind of food.

R eally it's a nice animal.

K ind not deadly sometimes.

Ben Maynes (7)
Hillside First School, Worle

Swordfish

S wordfish leap in and out

W hen swordfish go fast they are catching a fish

O n swordfish they have fins

R eally sharp nose

D o not touch it

F ast swordfish - 100 miles an hour

I n the sea

S omething that goes really fast

H ave you seen one?

Kyle Johnston-Smith (6)
Hillside First School, Worle

Stingray Poem

S wimming to the shore

T hey are grey, black and flat

I n the sea

N ever touch them, they sting

G ot to be camouflaged so the fish don't see it coming

R ays are different sizes

A stingray is dangerous

Y ou watch out for a stingray.

Harry Brueford (6)
Hillside First School, Worle

Fish Poem

F ish are different colours

I n the sea

S hiny scales

H ave orange and red scales.

Joshua Reeves (7)
Hillside First School, Worle

Doctor Who

D octor Who travels in time

O lympians are a race that never die

C ybermen and Daleks are The Doctor's enemies

T he TARDIS is his way of travelling

O pen wormholes the TARDIS travels through

R eaching galaxies that could be near you.

W hoever may need him

H e will be there

O nly Doctor Who will do.

Luke Taylor (6)
Kings Ash Primary School, Paignton

Doctor Who

D aleks are destroying the world.

O ff we go to a new planet.

C ybermen are coming to destroy them.

T here's a new Doctor coming to the planet.

O ff we go through space in a new planet.

R un away, the statues are coming.

W ho can save the world?

H ear a hero coming to save the world.

O h no Daleks are coming.

Ryan Mark Jones (7)
Kings Ash Primary School, Paignton

Doctor Who

D aleks destroy and devastate worlds

O n the horizon the TARDIS prevails

C hased through time and through different galaxies

T he Time Lord sets things back to reality

O n an adventure seeing wonders and more

R escuing worlds and damsels galore

W hen you need help he will be there

H elping you out when life is not fair

O verall Doctor Who does care.

Skye Shepherd (6)
Kings Ash Primary School, Paignton

69

Doctor Who

D octor Who is magic,

O n the lookout for Daleks,

C rashing through doors,

T ravelling through time,

O n a mission!

R unning as fast as we can.

W hat's around the corner?

H iding Daleks everywhere!

O nly Doctor Who can save the day!

Jasmine Gascoigne (5)
Kings Ash Primary School, Paignton

Doctor Who

D oing his best to save the world

O ut of the TARDIS

C atching the baddies as he goes

T icking time goes by fast

O pening the door and running out fast

R eady to catch

W eeping angels as they passed

H oping everything will work out

O pening his eyes and seeing the light of the night.

Harrison Blowers (5)
Kings Ash Primary School, Paignton

Doctor Who

D octor Who is a Time Lord

O n his TARDIS he flies

C hasing aliens around the world

T hrough the stars, the planets

O ften he has friends by his side

R ose, Martha, Amy, Sarah-Jane and K9

W ondering what adventure each day will bring

H e boldly goes where he is needed most

O nwards and upwards, he does everything but sing.

Phoebe Pestell (6)
Kings Ash Primary School, Paignton

Doctor Who

D octor and the Daleks

O ld and new enemies for you

C ybermen always causing trouble for you

T ARDIS blue, always there waiting for you

O ften here, there, everywhere, but nowhere

R emembering past, present and future

W hen time stands still you go on

H ow many trips you'll never know

O h Doctor where are thou?

Dakota Baldwin (5)
Kings Ash Primary School, Paignton

Doctor Who

D octor there's a problem somewhere

O ver on Earth you see

C elestial Intervention Agency sending The Doctor on missions

T ARDIS moves through the time/space vortex

O ne point the Time Lords try to escape

R ecurring monsters running all around

W eeping angels, who appear to be statues

H e hated war, he always did

O ver and out until another day.

Jay Dixon (5)
Kings Ash Primary School, Paignton

Doctor Who

D octor Who, Doctor Who

O h what

C an I do for you?

T ravelling, exploring

O r

R un to get your shoe

W here will you go?

H ow will you get there?

O n a TARDIS of blue.

Keisha Brookes (5)
Kings Ash Primary School, Paignton

Doctor Who

D octor Who is a TV programme

O f which produced by the BBC

C hasing time in his

T ime machine

O ften helping people and

R ighting wrongs

W ith his companions

H e explores

O uter space.

Yasmin Alder (5)
Kings Ash Primary School, Paignton

Doctor Who

D oors opening in the TARDIS

O perating the TARDIS

C hoosing course

T ime travelling

O n different planets

R ivalry of the Daleks

W aiting to land

H orrible aliens

O pen doors of TARDIS.

Tyler Cox (5)
Kings Ash Primary School, Paignton

73

Doctor Who

D aleks are your enemy
O pening ports to new worlds
C hasing iron men from their plans
T ravelling through time like no one else
O ffering help to those in need
R ose is your faithful friend

W atching out for evil all around
H elping Rose find her way home
O ften staring death in the face.

Alisha Collings (6)
Kings Ash Primary School, Paignton

Doctor Who

D octor Who
O ff on an adventure
C hasing the bad guys
T ravelling fast in his TARDIS
O n time to his friends
R unning to save the planet

W here to next?
H elp is on the way
O h thank you Doctor Who.

Joshua Squire (6)
Kings Ash Primary School, Paignton

Doctor Who

D aring to fight the world

O rders the aliens away

C rashing through the skies

T he TARDIS big and blue, spinning around

O pens doors to every world

R escuing people as he goes

W aiting until the aliens return

H e battles with the Daleks

O ften saving the world.

Angel Reeby (6)
Kings Ash Primary School, Paignton

Doctor Who

D aleks attack at every opportunity

O rganising planned attacks

C harging through time and space

T ravelling to unknown universes

O bstructing world domination

R escuing people in times of need

W aiting for the next mystery

H eroes amongst us all

O ffering protection against evil.

Luca Hailey (5)
Kings Ash Primary School, Paignton

Doctor Who

D ouble hearted time traveller

O verlooking all

C almly facing danger

T hrough the future and the past

O pening doors for many people

R iding in a TARDIS to get there in time

W ho could this be?

H ow is this so?

O h my gosh, it's Doctor Who.

Sophie Stothard (5)
Kings Ash Primary School, Paignton

William's Poem

W illiam loves football.

I like TV.

L ollipops are my favourite food.

L ots of fish at home.

I like to play on my Nintendo DS.

A lways playing rugby on Sunday

M y favourite colour is green.

William Flavin (6)
Lympsham CE (VC) First School, Lympsham

Jacob's Poem

J olly boy

A lways respectful

C at fighter

O bsessed with kung fu and

B ouncy too

J olly jumper

O beys the golden rules

N oisy too.

Jacob Nelson (7)
Lympsham CE (VC) First School, Lympsham

Laura's Poem

L aura is respectful and

A lways helpful. She is

U nforgettable and

R eally helpful

A nd grateful.

Laura Wade (5)
Lympsham CE (VC) First School, Lympsham

Tilly's Poem

T illy is my name.

I love my sister.

L illy is my friend.

L ots of clothes and toys.

Y ellow is my favourite colour.

B rilliant at reading.

O ften go swimming on Sunday.

L ibraries are fun.

E xcellent at writing.

Y o-yos are fun.

Tilly Boley (5)
Lympsham CE (VC) First School, Lympsham

Rio's Poem

R espectful child

I think in my head

O ther friends are nice to me.

Rio Brigden (6)
Lympsham CE (VC) First School, Lympsham

Kaitlin's Poem

K ind and helpful

A ctive and fit

I ntelligent and pretty

T rustful person and I love skipping

L oveable and

I love dogs

N ice and quiet girl.

Kaitlin Pettitt (6)
Lympsham CE (VC) First School, Lympsham

Eloise's Poem

E ating chocolate is what I like to do.

L oving Mummy is what I like to do.

O ld-fashioned wrapping is what I like to do.

I also like to run.

S miling all day is what I like to do.

E ating bananas is what I like to do.

Eloise Hopkins-O'Driscoll (6)
Lympsham CE (VC) First School, Lympsham

Charlotte's Poem

C ake is my favourite food.

H amsters are cool

A nd fluffy. I am

R espectful and give

L ove to my mum.

O ne day I would like to be a

T eacher and

T each art. I

E njoy art very much.

Charlotte Watson (7)
Lympsham CE (VC) First School, Lympsham

Mir's Poem

M arvellous Mir: I think I'm marvellous.

I ntelligent: I think I'm very intelligent.

R ight sometimes.

H ugger: I love hugging my mum and dad.

I rresistible: it's sooo irresistible to not eat chocolate.

C aring: I think I am caring.

K ind: I think I am kind.

S ophisticated: I think I am sophisticated.

O strich lover: I just love ostriches.

N ice: I think I am nice.

Mir Hickson (7)
Lympsham CE (VC) First School, Lympsham

Isabelle's Poem

I am helpful and

S uper with my friends. I

A m always kind. I like

B ells because they're shiny. I like

E dible presents. I like

L eeks and

L earning and doing

E xams for ballet.

Isabelle Carpenter (6)
Lympsham CE (VC) First School, Lympsham

Isabelle's Poem

I have a sister called Eleanor

S cientific and elegant

A lways kind and caring

B eing nice always to my sister

E ating fruit and veg all the time

L oving everyone at school and everywhere

L oving, hugging girl

E njoy PE.

Isabelle Clarke (5)
Lympsham CE (VC) First School, Lympsham

Ella's Poem

E xcellent at writing in school.

L ovely and enjoyable all the time.

L aughing at my dad's jokes.

A ble to write when I am at school.

Ella Hodgson (6)
Lympsham CE (VC) First School, Lympsham

Eve's Poem

E legant and beautiful.

V ery interested in pet shops.

E xcellent at ballet.

M arvellous at

A cting in a show.

R ight sometimes.

Y oung, I am only six.

Eve Hancock (6)
Lympsham CE (VC) First School, Lympsham

Angel's Poem

A ngel is pretty.

N ice a lot and friendly. I

G o dancing a lot.

E ating fruit is my favourite.

L aughing people all the time.

Angel Brooker (6)
Lympsham CE (VC) First School, Lympsham

Sam's Poem

S am is a kind boy.

A lways going to school.

M essing up my backroom when I'm at home.

Sam Crook (6)
Lympsham CE (VC) First School, Lympsham

Snow White

S he was a beautiful princess.

N ice to everyone.

O h how happy she was

W ith her dwarves.

W icked witch had an apple.

H ow did it get so dirty

I n the woods?

T his is a tiny house.

E ating the soup made her tired.

Fifi Collett (7)
Radipole Primary School, Weymouth

Snow White

S o beautiful.

N ice Snow White.

O ff to find the dwarves.

W icked witch gives her an apple.

W onderful.

H ow she wants a prince to rescue her.

I 'm a nice girl.

T he seven dwarves.

E verything happy.

Kieran Symes (6)
Radipole Primary School, Weymouth

Gingerbread Man

G iggling

I like him

N aughty man, very

G inger

'E ee,' he said to the oven

R unning fast

B e careful!

R acing mad

E veryone running

A lways bad and naughty

D ead at the end

M ad and crazy

A jolly guy

N ow he's gone!

Louis Hocking (6)
Radipole Primary School, Weymouth

Cinderella

C inderella is kind.

I think Cinderella got bored of the ugly sisters.

N ice and intelligent.

D ances with the prince at the ball!

E veryone looked pretty at the ball except the sisters.

R eally exciting time at the ball.

E xtremely poor.

L ovely girl!

L oves her friends!

A ll she wants is to go to the ball.

Amia Chalk (7)
Radipole Primary School, Weymouth

Three Pigs

T he pigs ran away from the

H ungry wolf.

R unning away from the nasty

E vil wolf.

E xtremely scared of the wolf.

P utting burning hot water under the chimney

I s a very clever plan.

'G o away,' shouted the pigs!

S o when the extremely good plan worked the pigs lived
happily ever after.

Oliver Pullin (7)
Radipole Primary School, Weymouth

Three Little Pigs

T he pigs were making a house.

H appy big pig because she got a brick house.

'R un,' went the little pig.

E ating porridge.

E ating bacon on the table.

L ittle pigs ran into Mummy's house.

I 'm scared.

T he busy three pigs are building.

T he naughty wolf.

L ook out for the wolf!

E nd was good for the pigs!

P ink pigs.

I like the pigs.

G o away wolf.

S teaming pot.

Alexander Barton (6)
Radipole Primary School, Weymouth

The Three Pigs

T he pigs ran away from the wolf

H ouses of straw, wood and bricks

E ating porridge in the straw

T he two houses of straw and wood are blown down

'H ungry,' said piggy 1.

'R unning away from the wolf,' said the piggy 3.

'E ating porridge is my favourite,' said piggy 1.

'E ating bread is my favourite,' said piggy 1.

P iggy number 1 said, 'The bread is nice.'

'I tried to blow down the houses,' said the wolf.

'G o away bad wolf.'

S ad wolf because he got his bottom burnt.

Nicole Barber (6)
Radipole Primary School, Weymouth

Buttons

B uttons is a butler.

U ndid the letter from

T he King and Queen.

T here are lots of letters

O n the doorstep for Buttons.

N ever breaks friends with Cinderella.

S ometimes helps Cinderella.

Jessica Mutch (7)
Radipole Primary School, Weymouth

Cinderella

C leans all the furniture

I n her dreams she wants to go to the ball

N ice person

D anced like a princess

E nd of the ball she ran home!

R osy cheeks

E xcited

L ovely time

L ooking pretty in her dress

A happy girl.

William Dennis (6)
Radipole Primary School, Weymouth

The Three Pigs

T he pigs were building their

H ouse!

E ach house made out of different materials.

T he bad wolf came.

H uff, puff, the wolf blew their houses down.

R un away quick!

E ek, pig 2 was scared.

E ek, pig 1 was scared too.

P ig 3 said, 'Don't be a scaredy-cat.'

I t's lunchtime,' said the wolf.

'G o, go wolf,'

S aid the pigs.

Chloe Hughes-Taylor (6)
Radipole Primary School, Weymouth

Three Little Pigs

T ough and brave when they made their house

H ungry all the time

R ough sometimes

E ating the coarse hay sometimes

E xtremely messy

L ovely and pink, they are quite

I nteresting

T rying to get out their home all the time

T hey love pig food

L ove pig food

E at grapes as well as pig food

P leasant not

I rritable

G rumpy and

S melly.

Jamie Cleaver (6)
Radipole Primary School, Weymouth

Cinderella

C ommotion all the time.

I mportant job to do.

N obody did their own work but Cinderella.

D reaming of meeting the prince.

E very day she's cleaning.

R eady by 7am every day.

E ar to ear she listens.

L arge piles of washing to do.

L ots of mess on the floor.

A lways working her socks off.

Emma Wood (7)
Radipole Primary School, Weymouth

Cinderella

C inderella is sad

I wish to go to the ball

N ew dress

D reams come true

E veryone dances now

R abbits are friends

E veryone looks beautiful

L ook who's there

L ovely prince

A clock strikes 12.

Daniel Corps (7)
Radipole Primary School, Weymouth

Peter Pan

P irates everywhere.

E arrings on every pirate.

T errified Peter.

E nemies firing at Peter.

R escuing the Lost Boys.

P eter ducking and diving.

A lligator eats Captain Hook.

N everland is where Peter Pan lives!

George Cartwright (7)
Radipole Primary School, Weymouth

Cinderella

C an't go to the ball.

I mpossible to tidy up.

N ice animals come to help.

D ancing fairy godmother comes.

E smeralda and Griselda come back.

R unning Cinderella came back.

E nchanting prince appears looking for her.

L oves going dancing.

L ate night coming back.

A fter all she marries the prince.

Monica Merritt (6)
Radipole Primary School, Weymouth

Cinderella

C inderella is sad

I wish to go to a ball

N ew dress

D reams come true

E veryone dances

R abbits are friends

E veryone dances

L ook who's here

L ovely prince

A clock strikes 12.

Lewis Chalker (6)
Radipole Primary School, Weymouth

Goldilocks

G oldilocks off for a walk

O pens the three bears' door

L ooks at the steaming porridge

D oesn't hesitate

I nto the bedroom she goes

L ies on the little bed

O h no, the three bears come home!

C hase Goldilocks away

K eeping their door locked

S o Goldilocks can't come back.

Charlie Gledhill (6)
Radipole Primary School, Weymouth

Cinderella

C inderella is very tired.

I n and out sweeping and cleaning.

N ever has any fun.

D reaming of meeting the prince.

E verybody takes no notice of her.

R escued by fairy godmother.

E nough of cleaning and off to the ball.

L ate for the ball.

L ovely dancing with Prince Charming.

A s the clock strikes 12 she runs home.

Mailia Brown (6)
Radipole Primary School, Weymouth

Cinderella

C inderella had to do all of the work.

I 'm tired of all the work.

N asty ugly sisters and brothers.

D irty clothes for Cinderella to clean.

E verybody makes her clean up.

R eally sad.

E veryone has gone to the ball.

L ots of dancing.

L ots of people

A nd Cinderella loses her shoe.

Hannah Stanhope (7)
Radipole Primary School, Weymouth

Chocolate

C hocolate is delicious

H eated chocolate is yummy

O range chocolate

C runchy chocolate

O nly one chocolate allowed a day

L umpy chocolate

A ny chocolate

T asty and yummy

E very type of chocolate.

Stephen Gliddon (7)
St John's School, Sidmouth

Chocolates

C hocolates are creamy

H eating it is fun

O nly one should you have

C ooler than a bun

O range is yucky

L ovely chocolate though

A lthough try and guess my favourite

T asty and yummy

E at them all

S trawberry! How did you guess?

Isabel Williams (7)
St John's School, Sidmouth

My Older Brother

R ick works

I n the garage

C arefully fixing cars

K itKat he loves at his break.

Angelica Hellinikakis (7)
St John's School, Sidmouth

My Friend

C leo is confident with her work.

L ikes Molly.

E ats spaghetti and

O ats in flapjacks she likes.

Adam Stratton-Keay (7)
St John's School, Sidmouth

My Brother

C leab is cool, he's

L ike my best brother,

E very day he plays

A t football matches

B ut he always wins.

Noah Innes-Kruger (6)
St John's School, Sidmouth

My Dog

P olo is sweet and

O il hurts her fur.

L ovely little puppy and

O n the hills she runs.

Cleo Turley (6)
St John's School, Sidmouth

My Friend

C areful Cleo

L ikes playing with her friends

E ating fast

O nly likes me when we are friendly.

Molly Bowker (6)
St John's School, Sidmouth

My Pet

C harlie is very naughty

H is tail is a shorty

A pples he hates

R abbits he chases

L ying he loves but

I tching is his favourite hobby

E rin is his favourite.

Erin Kirley (7)
St John's School, Sidmouth

My Friend's Brother

C aleb is cool

A nd clumsy

L ions he likes and

E ach time he has to run

B ut sometimes he gets back home.

Miles Lewis (6)
St John's School, Sidmouth

Georgina

G reen light to go

E ating chicken nuggets tastes good

O range is my favourite colour

R oses are red

G rapes are my favourite fruit

I n the night it is a black sky

N uts taste horrible

A pples are crunchy.

Georgina Medlicott (6)
St Joseph's Catholic Primary School, Highweek

Madison

M y friend is fun.

A pples are delicious.

D ad is nice to me.

I love Mum and Dad.

S weets are the best.

O ranges are fruit.

N ice friends make me happy.

Madie Breslan-Dore (7)
St Joseph's Catholic Primary School, Highweek

Cody

C ars drive on the roads

O ranges grow on trees

D o not like going to bed

Y ucky cabbage.

Cody Phillips (6)
St Joseph's Catholic Primary School, Highweek

Harriet Duke

H orses
A nts
R ed
R unning
I ngsdon
E llis
T rials

D inosaurs
U gbrooke
K nights
E lephant.

Harriet Duke (6)
St Joseph's Catholic Primary School, Highweek

Alex

A mber is my favourite colour
L ollipops are my favourite food
E llis is my friend
X -rays make sure bones are not broken.

Alex Stackhouse (5)
St Joseph's Catholic Primary School, Highweek

Patrick

P urple is yucky.

A pples are yummy.

T apping on a table.

R unning is my favourite sport.

I like playing with my friends.

C ircle time is funny.

K nights are scary.

Patrick Warren (6)
St Joseph's Catholic Primary School, Highweek

Faith

F unny fish

A fluffy coat

I love my cuddly

T ennis I enjoy watching

H opping happy.

Faith Stevens (5)
St Joseph's Catholic Primary School, Highweek

Play For Fun!

T yler loves play.

Y o-yos swing and bounce.

L ovely lime squash.

E asy peasy games.

R oly polies are fun.

Tyler Ridgment (6)
St Mellion CE (VA) School, St Mellion

My Poem

H annah likes DSi

A nd watching movies

N oodles are nice

N ests are pretty

A mazing swimming

H orses are cute, rabbits too.

H amsters are noisy

A stronauts are freaky

L ittle puppies are adorable

L ollies are lovely.

Hannah Hall (6)
St Mellion CE (VA) School, St Mellion

Hello Kitty

E llie likes dolphins

L ibby is crazy

L ucie likes dogs

I ce creams are cold

E llie likes Hello Kitty.

Ellie Royston (5)
St Mellion CE (VA) School, St Mellion

Big Cat

H arvey is happy

A happy Harvey

R ed is my favourite colour

V olcano blast

E agle flies over

Y oghurts are yummy.

Harvey Nye (6)
St Mellion CE (VA) School, St Mellion

Holly's Poem

H olly is monstrous like a dinosaur.

O therwise very beautiful.

L ots of people like her.

L ion-like but lovely.

Y ou want the real her - this is it!

C hoosing is her favourite.

H olly likes sharks and Ice Age.

A nd fairy tales.

D ancing and dragons.

W itches and princesses.

I ce Age the film.

C lass 1 is the best.

K now that!

Holly Chadwick (6)
St Mellion CE (VA) School, St Mellion

Big Ben

B en likes to go to school

E ven more than home

N ot as much as writing

P erhaps I will play my DS

I slands are good to explore in

T axis take you places

M en are big

A nd caterpillars are long

N ot as tall as a giraffe.

Ben Pitman (6)
St Mellion CE (VA) School, St Mellion

James

J elly makes me happy

A nd I like football

M um bought me a watch

E lephants have big feet

S o I really like soldiers.

James Dawe (6)
St Mellion CE (VA) School, St Mellion

Dylan James

D ylan likes dogs.

Y oghurts are tasty.

L ions love logs.

A mbulances are hasty.

N ests are warm.

J ourneys are funny.

A pples are crunchy.

M ums are clever.

E lephants are big.

S nakes are great.

Dylan Rundle (5)
St Mellion CE (VA) School, St Mellion

Abi Royston

A bi likes swimming

B ears play in the woods

I nsects are creepy.

R abbits are cute

O ctopus slide

Y oghurts you can eat

S nowmen are cold

T V is fun to watch

O ranges are squishy

N oah had an ark.

Abi Royston (7)
St Mellion CE (VA) School, St Mellion

My Poem About Me

L ibby likes the Wii

I ce creams are yummy

B utterflies are pretty

B alls are colourful

Y o-yos are fun

C ars are fast

O wls are cute

N ests are big

W ind is noisy

A nts tickle

Y oghurts taste nice.

Libby Conway (6)
St Mellion CE (VA) School, St Mellion

My Lovely Animals

R abbits and puppies are very cute.

U gly ones I like too.

B utterflies and ladybirds look pretty in the air.

Y es I do like insects too.

C ats have babies and they are called kittens.

A nts are very tiny and small.

R acoons climb very tall trees

D ogs look cute when they're asleep.

E lephants are big and grey.

W hen I think of animals I smile very happily.

Ruby Loveday Cardew (7)
St Mellion CE (VA) School, St Mellion

My Teacher!

M iss Trickey is tricky

I nteresting

S he teaches us maths and stuff

S mart

T eaches us swimming and more

R eads with us

I t's great having Miss Trickey as a teacher

C lever

K ind

E xcellent

Y ou're lots of fun!

Esme Marshall (6)
Shaftesbury CE Primary School, Shaftesbury

Me

A mazing

L ike my new cup?

I like ice

S aturday is my favourite

H ugging my sister

A dventures I love.

Alisha Headlong (6)
Shaftesbury CE Primary School, Shaftesbury

Dogs

D oze
O n the sofa
G rowl
S mall.

Hayden Goodship (6)
Shaftesbury CE Primary School, Shaftesbury

Cats

C uddle
A ttack
T ickle
S nap.

Athene Viner (6)
Shaftesbury CE Primary School, Shaftesbury

Harry

H urrying to rugby
A ll of my friends
R ugby for North Dorset
R unning and skidding
Y es, I scored a try!

Harry Hunt (6)
Shaftesbury CE Primary School, Shaftesbury

Penguins

P enguins are furry as you stroke them
E nergetic as you watch them
N ice as you watch them diving and eating fish
G et them turning diving down to get fish
U mbrella hiding underneath
I n the Antarctic frozen solid
N aughty penguins.

Millie Boughtwood (7)
Shaftesbury CE Primary School, Shaftesbury

Camel

C ute

A hump

M ucky

E asily

L ike grass.

Chelsea Oram-Gaertig (6)
Shaftesbury CE Primary School, Shaftesbury

Cats

C uddly

A ttack

T iny

S oft.

Lewis Kendall (7)
Shaftesbury CE Primary School, Shaftesbury

Cats

C uddly

A ttack

T ails

S pecial.

Megan Scammell (6)
Shaftesbury CE Primary School, Shaftesbury

Cheetah

C aterpillars are slow

H uskies howl

E legant babies

E lephants are big

T ortoises are great

A nts are little

H uskies bark.

Blake Horwood (6)
Shaftesbury CE Primary School, Shaftesbury

Lion

L oud

I tchy

O n me

N aughty.

Jordan-Leah Bates (6)
Shaftesbury CE Primary School, Shaftesbury

Lion

L ying around

I nside

O ver there

N aughty.

Ryan Danson (7)
Shaftesbury CE Primary School, Shaftesbury

Giraffe

G iraffe
I nteresting
R un
A nimals
F ast
F emale
E at leaves.

Emily Ingram (7)
Shaftesbury CE Primary School, Shaftesbury

Dogs

D ogs
O r walks
G o
S ausage dog.

Joshua Brady (6)
Shaftesbury CE Primary School, Shaftesbury

Henry

H enry is horrid

E nergetic

N ice to play with

R otten as well

Y elling at his friends!

Henry White (7)
Shaftesbury CE Primary School, Shaftesbury

My Name

E xtra special to my family.

L aughing all the tIme.

L ively every day.

A dventurous and playful.

W illing to have a go.

I have a pet dog called Jack.

L ovely to all my friends.

L ike to go to school.

S unny and bright.

Ella Wills (6)
Stoberry Park School, Wells

My Name

B eautiful and caring.

O nly young.

N eat and tidy.

N ice to my friends.

I mportant to my family.

E verything is fun!

B rilliant at maths.

Bonnie Bale (6)
Stoberry Park School, Wells

My Name

S mart and intelligent.

E ats cottage pie.

B eautiful smile.

H anging out with my best friend is fun.

Seb Hopes (7)
Stoberry Park School, Wells

My Name

F un and fair.

R eady to learn at all times.

E xploring is my favourite game.

D reaming of what I can be?

B en is my best friend.

Fred Blair (6)
Stoberry Park School, Wells

My Name

H elpful and kind.

A cting is my ambition.

Z zzz . . . I like to dream.

E njoy eating delicious fruit.

L ovely and pretty.

P lay nicely with my friends.

Hazel Pearcey (5)
Stoberry Park School, Wells

My Name

M atthew is my name
A sh is my class
T ry my best
T ired at times
H elping others
E njoy reading
W illing to learn.

Matthew Hodson (6)
Stoberry Park School, Wells

My Name

R ead to learn.
O pen to new ideas.
S uper at art.
I nterested in everything.
E veryone's friend and always smiling.

Rosie Jones (6)
Stoberry Park School, Wells

My Name

S miley and sweet.

A lways so happy.

M uddy when playing.

J olly with my friends.

Sam Jukes (5)
Stoberry Park School, Wells

My Name

M errily going along.

E xpress.

G irly by nature.

A ffectionate and helpful.

N ice and kind to my friends.

Megan Laws (6)
Stoberry Park School, Wells

My Name

J olly and bright.

E nthusiastic to learn.

S weet and kind.

S miley every day.

I ntelligent at school.

C aring to my friends.

A lways happy.

Jessica Stevens (6)
Stoberry Park School, Wells

My Name

L ovely and friendly.

I ntelligent and hard-working.

L ittle animals make me smile.

Y oung and sweet.

W onderful and wise.

E nthusiastic to learn.

B e the best you can . . .

B e.

Lily Webb (7)
Stoberry Park School, Wells

My Name

M aking is fun.

I love my family.

C aring.

H appy.

A lways try.

E njoy Star Wars.

L ovely.

Michael Moore (5)
Stoberry Park School, Wells

My Name

K ind to everyone.

A ctive and adventurous.

S pecial to my family.

E ats pasta.

Y oung at six years old.

H appy and smiley.

Kasey Hares (6)
Stoberry Park School, Wells

My Name

H appy and cheerful.

O pen to help.

L iked by my friends.

L earning is fun.

I nterested to read.

E ats eggs.

Hollie Wallace (5)
Stoberry Park School, Wells

My Name

L ovely Laurie is seven.

A lways try my best.

U p and running.

R unning is my favourite thing.

I have a dog called Flossie.

E nergetic.

Laurie Rastogi (6)
Stoberry Park School, Wells

Joel

J okey

O ldest brother

E xercise

L aughing.

Joel Fowler (5)
Stoberry Park School, Wells

Georgina

G reen eyes.

E very day I walk to school.

O range is my favourite colour.

R ules are important to me.

G oing to school is important to me.

I have a baby brother.

N o one knows my dog yet.

A lovely day today isn't it?

Georgina Collins
Stoberry Park School, Wells

Jamie Jordan

J umping expert.

A cool boy.

M assive.

I love school.

E at fast.

J ump high.

O ff I go fast.

R ide my bike fast.

D eadly.

A strong boy.

N o one bothers me.

Jamie Jordan
Stoberry Park School, Wells

Freya May

F reya is funny.

R ed squirrels are my favourite animal.

E xcited at parties.

Y ellow-haired girl who works as hard as she can.

A s happy as a bee.

M ay be polite at parties.

A s polite to be happy.

Y oghurts would be good for me.

Freya Jukes (7)
Stoberry Park School, Wells

Ben

B en has green eyes.

E xcellent at flying my helicopter.

N oisy every day.

Ben Thompson (7)
Stoberry Park School, Wells

Zoe Liling

Z ebras are my favourite animal

O ranges are juicy and my favourite fruit

E lephants are big

L eave me alone

I gloos are cold

L eave my sister alone

I nvite my friend to a party

N ails are sharp

G eorgina has lots of friends.

Zoe Pao (6)
Stoberry Park School, Wells

Aidan

A idan is my name
I like ice cream
D arren's my dad
A pples are yummy
N anny is good.

Aidan Nosworthy (6)
Stoberry Park School, Wells

Hannah

H appy I am
A nd long hair
N ice to my friends
N ice to my family
A nd friendly
H ot and cold.

Hannah Ruddle
Stoberry Park School, Wells

Tyler

T oys
Y ellow
L ove my skateboard
E ggs are good for me
R abbits.

Tyler Lane (6)
Stoberry Park School, Wells

Georgina

G loves
E xplaining
O ranges
R oses are beautiful
G eorgina has fun at school
I like being in Willow class
N ight-time is beautiful
A pples are good for me.

Georgina Selby (7)
Stoberry Park School, Wells

Beau

B owling is good for me

E xercise keeps me fit

A pples are a good fruit for me

U mbrellas keep me dry.

Beau Jay (6)
Stoberry Park School, Wells

Finlay

F in I am.

I have blue eyes.

N ot ticklish at all.

L uckier than ever.

A mazing because unusual name.

Y o-yos can't really do anything.

Fin Sherman (7)
Stoberry Park School, Wells

Courtney

C ry when my sister is mean to me

O ranges are my favourite fruit and banana cake

U gly dogs I do not like

R ed roses are so pretty, I always pick some for my mum.

T ea is very yummy in my tummy

N ext I go to sleep

E ggs are delicious

Y ummy, yummy crumpets for my breakfast.

Courtney Legresley (7)
Stoberry Park School, Wells

Deacon

D oesn't like Mars bars.

E aster egg hunt lover.

A mazing at science.

C ool dude.

O ne day I want to be a scientist.

N ice and funny person.

Deacon Montgomery (6)
Stoberry Park School, Wells

Kelly

K ind sister really.

E ats spaghetti Bolognese.

L ikes yellow

L oves mee mow and mee mow

Y esterday I saw the police.

Kelly Higgins (5)
Stoberry Park School, Wells

Freya

F un and friendly.

R eally likes to make things.

E very Thursday I go to country dancing.

Y esterday some police came.

A lways happy and silly.

Freya Barton-Hine (6)
Stoberry Park School, Wells

Emilia

E milia adores enormous elephants.

M y goldfish are called Emilie and Mathyus.

I like juicy apples.

L ike little lollipops.

I love school.

A mazing girl.

Emilia Wilson (6)
Stoberry Park School, Wells

Kyle

K ind and friendly.

Y ellow isn't my favourite colour.

L ovely black trousers.

E at broccoli.

Kyle Blake (5)
Stoberry Park School, Wells

Kenneth

K en loves cats

E ggs I like

N ests I like

N ight-time I like

E ating I like

T alking I like

H appy I like.

Kenneth Greenshields (5)
Stoberry Park School, Wells

Jessica

J ess is lovely

E very day I'm excited

S he's got blonde hair

S he's got a hat on

I go to school in the morning

C rying Jess falling over

A pples I like.

Jessica Roberts-Lewis (6)
Stoberry Park School, Wells

Tyler

T oby is my best friend.

Y ellow is my favourite colour.

L ike to watch TV.

E gg is my favourite food.

R eally like crisps.

Tyler Elms (7)
Stoberry Park School, Wells

Joel

J ogging I like

O pening presents

E ggs I don't like

L ily is my sister.

Joel Webb (6)
Stoberry Park School, Wells

Adam

A nts I like.

D inosaurs I like.

A nimals I like.

M aking models I like.

Adam Robinson (5)
Stoberry Park School, Wells

Charles

C harming

H airy

A m happy

R eally like swimming

L ike pizza

E dward is my brother

S uper at football.

Charles Benson (6)
Stoberry Park School, Wells

Caitlin

C aitlin's best friend is Charlotte
A t the weekend I went to the park
I have two cats and they are cute
T hings that I did with my daddy
L ove dogs and cats
I am good at diabolo
N ever been for a sleepover.

Caitlin Baker (7)
Stoberry Park School, Wells

Yummy Honey

H oney is sweet
O ld honey is dry
N ew honey is sticky
E very honey is
Y ummy!

Ross Oliver Hopkins (6)
The Abbey CE (VA) Primary School, Shaftesbury

Tropical Island

I sland rocks are as solid as iron

S and as soft as a very perfect cloud

L ovely sights of the sea

A moon as bright as a crystal

N ature, nature all around

D ig in the cloudy sand

S eas to swim in as salty as they are!

Aron Walter (6)
The Abbey CE (VA) Primary School, Shaftesbury

All About Me!

E specially likes dinosaurs.

L earns about lands.

L ike a lion cub with her ginger hair.

I ce cream is one of her favourite foods.

C aught a caterpillar in a playground.

I cicles she likes because she saw a massive one.

A lligators she's always wanted to see.

Ellicia Gosling (7)
The Abbey CE (VA) Primary School, Shaftesbury

Tess

T ess can sing beautifully.

E njoys running quickly.

S miley as can be.

S uper at swimming.

Tess Howarth-Jones (7)
The Abbey CE (VA) Primary School, Shaftesbury

Teachers

T eachers teach.

E nergetic games.

A nd sleep.

C hat a lot.

H ead teacher is boss!

E very teacher teaches.

R eally good games.

Billy Lewis (6)
The Abbey CE (VA) Primary School, Shaftesbury

Jessica

J oyful Jessica is very beautiful.

E specially likes ponies.

S uper at literacy.

S he is sensible.

I magines a lot.

C ares about a lot of people.

A fantastic violinist.

Jessica Sverdloff (7)
The Abbey CE (VA) Primary School, Shaftesbury

Teagan

T errific at running.

E xcited about my new book.

A ctive at PE.

G iggles lots of the time.

A rtistic at painting.

N ibbles apples.

Teagan Nicholls (5)
Trythall Community Primary School, New Mill

Kaelin

K ind and caring.

A mazing footballer.

E xtremely polite.

L ong legs.

I nteresting player.

N ice boy.

Kaelin Metcalfe (6)
Trythall Community Primary School, New Mill

Kit

K icking the ball in the net is exciting.

I diotic and annoying sometimes.

T errific at maths always!

Kit Renshaw-Hammond (5)
Trythall Community Primary School, New Mill

Mia

M arvellous cook.

I nteresting dancer.

A mazing artist.

Mia Roberts Drew (5)
Trythall Community Primary School, New Mill

Robin

R obin running in the woods.

O bstacles are fun.

B ouncing on my trampoline.

I like playing at playtime.

N oisy all the time!

Robin Burton (7)
Trythall Community Primary School, New Mill

Sennen

S uperb and smart.

E xcited about rugby.

N ever wrong!

N ext year I will be eight.

E xcellent at surfing.

N early off to Florida.

Sennen Laing (7)
Trythall Community Primary School, New Mill

Robert

R unning fast downhill!

O range hater.

B uilds super models.

E xcitable.

R eally funny.

T oy Story lover.

Robert Prowse (7)
Trythall Community Primary School, New Mill

Katie

K ittens love me.

A nd I like cuddles.

T homas is my brother.

I have a tabby cat.

E veryone loves me.

Katie Mansfield (5)
Wellesley Park Primary School, Wellington

Gemma

G oes to school happy.

E lephants are my favourite animals.

M y dog is lively.

M y dog licks everyone.

A very good dancer.

Gemma Rudd (6)
Wellesley Park Primary School, Wellington

Brooke

B rilliant at football.

R eally good at dancing.

O ranges are my favourite fruit.

O range is my favourite colour.

K eeps smiling all the time.

E ats all the time.

Brooke Aspin (5)
Wellesley Park Primary School, Wellington

Lily

L oves zebras.

I nterested in animals.

L emons are my favourite fruit.

Y oghurts are yummy.

Lily Hughes (5)
Wellesley Park Primary School, Wellington

Macsen

My mum feeds me different food.

And watches television with me.

Cricket is really fun.

Spiders frighten me.

Edward is my best friend.

Nearly six years old.

Macsen Hughes (5)
Wellesley Park Primary School, Wellington

Young Writers Information

We hope you have enjoyed reading this book - and that you will continue to enjoy it in the coming years.

If you like reading and writing poetry drop us a line, or give us a call, and we'll send you a free information pack.

Alternatively if you would like to order further copies of this book or any of our other titles, then please give us a call or log onto our website at www.youngwriters.co.uk.

Young Writers Information
Remus House
Coltsfoot Drive
Peterborough
PE2 9BF
(01733) 890066